Romans

A Latin-English,
Verse-by-Verse Translation

Translated by John Cunyus

ISBN# 978-1-936497-04-1

Latin text from *Biblia Sacra Iuxta Vulgatam Versionem*,
Fourth Revised Edition, edited by Roger Gryson,
© 1994 Deutsche Bibelgesellschaft, Stuttgart.
Used by permission.

Scripture citations in the footnotes are from
the Authorized (King James) Version.

Searchlight Press
Who are you looking for?
Publishers of thoughtful Christian books since 1994.
5634 Ledgestone Drive
Dallas, TX 75214-2026
888.896.6081
info@Searchlight-Press.com
www.Searchlight-Press.com
www.JohnCunyus.com

To Wayne and Mable Davee

Salutation

Romans 1:1 *Paulus servus Christi Iesu vocatus apostolus segregatus in evangelium Dei*

Paul, Christ Jesus's slave, called *an* apostle, set apart in God's good news,

1:2 *quod ante promiserat per prophetas suos in scripturis sanctis*

which He had promised before through His prophets, in holy writings

1:3 *de Filio suo qui factus est ex semine David secundum carnem*

about His Son: who came from David's seed according to flesh;

1:4 *qui praedestinatus est Filius Dei in virtute secundum Spiritum sanctificationis ex resurrectione mortuorum Iesu Christi Domini nostri*

who was predestined *as* God's Son in might, according to sanctification's Spirit, by *the* resurrection of Jesus Christ our Lord from *the* dead;

1:5 *per quem accepimus gratiam et apostolatum ad*

oboediendum fidei in omnibus gentibus pro nomine eius

through whom we have received grace and apostleship to faith's obedience among all nations, for His name;

1:6 *in quibus estis et vos vocati Iesu Christi*

in whom you also are called in Jesus Christ:

1:7 *omnibus qui sunt Romae dilectis Dei vocatis sanctis gratia vobis et pax a Deo Patre nostro et Domino Iesu Christo*

to all who are in Rome, loved of God, called holy. Grace to you and peace from God our Father and *the* Lord Jesus Christ.

Thanks
1:8 *primum quidem gratias ago Deo meo per Iesum Christum pro omnibus vobis quia fides vestra adnuntiatur in universo mundo*

First, indeed, I give thanks to my God through Jesus Christ for all of you, because your faith is told in all *the* world.

1:9 *testis enim mihi est Deus cui servio in spiritu meo in evangelio Filii eius quod sine intermissione memoriam vestri facio*

For God, whom I serve in my spirit and in His Son's good news, is witness to me that I make memory of you without ceasing,

1:10 *semper in orationibus meis obsecrans si quo modo tandem aliquando prosperum iter habeam in voluntate Dei veniendi ad vos*

pleading always in my prayers if somehow, at last, I may have *a* successful way in God's will to come to you.

Paul's Desire
to See the Romans

1:11 *desidero enim videre vos ut aliquid inpertiar gratiae vobis spiritalis ad confirmandos vos*

For I have wanted to see you, so I might share some spiritual grace with you, to strengthen you –

1:12 *id est simul consolari in vobis per eam quae invicem est fidem vestram atque meam*

that is, to be consoled together among you, through

that which is in turn your faith and mine.

1:13 *nolo autem vos ignorare fratres quia saepe proposui venire ad vos et prohibitus sum usque adhuc ut aliquem fructum habeam et in vobis sicut et in ceteris gentibus*

But I don't want you ignorant, brothers, that I have often proposed to come to you – and up to now have been prevented – that I may have some fruit also among you, as also among other nations.

Debtor to Greek
and Barbarian

1:14 *Graecis ac barbaris sapientibus et insipientibus debitor sum*

I am debtor to Greeks and barbarians, wise and foolish,

1:15 *ita quod in me promptum est et vobis qui Romae estis evangelizare*

so that in me *it* is ready to evangelize also among you who are in Rome.

The Gospel's Purpose

1:16 *non enim erubesco evangelium virtus enim Dei*

est in salutem omni credenti Iudaeo primum et Graeco

For I am not ashamed of *the* good news. For it is God's might to *the* well-being of every believer: Jew first, and Greek.

1:17 *iustitia enim Dei in eo revelatur ex fide in fidem sicut scriptum est iustus autem ex fide vivit*

For God's fairness is made clear in it, from faith to faith, as is written: "But *the* fair *one* lives from faith."[1]

1:18 *revelatur enim ira Dei de caelo super omnem impietatem et iniustitiam hominum eorum qui veritatem in iniustitiam detinent*

For God's anger is revealed from *the* sky over every human lawlessness and unfairness, of those who hold back truth in unfairness –

1:19 *quia quod notum est Dei manifestum est in illis Deus enim illis manifestavit*

---

[1] Habakkuk 2:4. Behold, his soul which is lifted up is not upright in him: but the just shall live by his faith.

because what is known of God is clear to them, for God made it clear to them.

Inexcusable Ignorance

1:20 *invisibilia enim ipsius a creatura mundi per ea quae facta sunt intellecta conspiciuntur sempiterna quoque eius virtus et divinitas ut sint inexcusabiles*

For His invisible *wonders* are seen, understood from *the* world's creation through those things that are made – His might and divinity, likewise – so they may be inexcusable!

1:21 *quia cum cognovissent Deum non sicut Deum glorificaverunt aut gratias egerunt sed evanuerunt in cogitationibus suis et obscuratum est insipiens cor eorum*

Because when they had known God, they did not glorify *Him* as God or give thanks. But they became vain in their schemings and their foolish heart was darkened.

1:22 *dicentes enim se esse sapientes stulti facti sunt*

For, claiming themselves to be wise, they became fools,

1:23 *et mutaverunt gloriam incorruptibilis Dei in similitudinem imaginis corruptibilis hominis et volucrum et quadrupedum et serpentium*

and they changed *the* incorruptible God's glory into *the* likeness of *a* corruptible image – of *a* human, or of flying *beings*, or four-legged *animals*, or snakes.

1:24 *propter quod tradidit illos Deus in desideria cordis eorum in inmunditiam ut contumeliis adficiant corpora sua in semet ipsis*

For this reason, God handed them over to their heart's desires to uncleanness, that they may afflict their bodies by abuse among themselves –

1:25 *qui commutaverunt veritatem Dei in mendacio et coluerunt et servierunt creaturae potius quam creatori qui est benedictus in saecula amen*

who changed God's truth into *a* lie, and worshiped and served *the* creature more than *the* Creator, who is blessed in *the* age. Amen.

1:26 *propterea tradidit illos Deus in passiones ignominiae nam feminae eorum inmutaverunt naturalem usum in eum usum qui est contra naturam*

Because of this, God handed them over to shameful passions. For their females exchanged natural use into that use which is against nature.

1:27 *similiter autem et masculi relicto naturali usu feminae exarserunt in desideriis suis in invicem masculi in masculos turpitudinem operantes et mercedem quam oportuit erroris sui in semet ipsis recipientes*

And males likewise, abandoning *the* natural use of *the* female, burned in their desires for one another, males working shame in males and receiving in themselves *the* reward that must come from their errors.

1:28 *et sicut non probaverunt Deum habere in notitia tradidit eos Deus in reprobum sensum ut faciant quae non conveniunt*

And since they did not approve of having God in notice, God handed them over to *a* base sense, so they may do what ought not *be done,*

1:29 *repletos omni iniquitate malitia fornicatione avaritia nequitia plenos invidia homicidio contentione dolo malignitate susurrones*

filled by every treachery: malice, fornication, greed,

worthlessness; filled with envy, murder, contention, deceit, ill-will; gossipers,

1:30 *detractores Deo odibiles contumeliosos superbos elatos inventores malorum parentibus non oboedientes*

disparagers, haters of God, quarrelers; proud, conceited, inventors of harm; not obeying parents;

1:31 *insipientes inconpositos sine affectione absque foedere sine misericordia*

unmade fools, without affection, without faith, without mercy –

1:32 *qui cum iustitiam Dei cognovissent non intellexerunt quoniam qui talia agunt digni sunt morte non solum ea faciunt sed et consentiunt facientibus*

who, when they had known God's fairness, did not understand that those doing such things are worthy of death – not only *those* who are doing them, but *those who* approve of those doing them.

Inexcusable Judging

Romans 2:1 *propter quod inexcusabilis es o homo omnis qui iudicas in quo enim iudicas alterum te ipsum condemnas eadem enim agis qui iudicas*

Because of this, you are inexcusable, O man, everyone who judges, for in what you judge another, you condemn yourself. For you who judge are carrying on *the* same *way*.

2:2 *scimus enim quoniam iudicium Dei est secundum veritatem in eos qui talia agunt*

For we know that judgment according to truth is God's, to those who carry on in such *ways*.

2:3 *existimas autem hoc o homo qui iudicas eos qui talia agunt et facis ea quia tu effugies iudicium Dei*

But do you consider this, O man – you who judge those who carry on in such *ways* and you do them – that you will avoid God's judgment?

2:4 *an divitias bonitatis eius et patientiae et longanimitatis contemnis ignorans quoniam benignitas Dei ad paenitentiam te adducit*

Or do you condemn *the* riches of His goodness and

patience and longsuffering, not knowing that God's kindness leads you to penitence?

2:5 *secundum duritiam autem tuam et inpaenitens cor thesaurizas tibi iram in die irae et revelationis iusti iudicii Dei*

But according to your hardness and impenitent heart, you are storing up for yourself anger on *the* day of anger and *the* revelation of God's fair judgment,

2:6 *qui reddet unicuique secundum opera eius*

who will repay to each one according to his works:

2:7 *his quidem qui secundum patientiam boni operis gloriam et honorem et incorruptionem quaerentibus vitam aeternam*

glory and honor and deathlessness indeed to those who, according to patience in good works, are seeking eternal life;

2:8 *his autem qui ex contentione et qui non adquiescunt veritati credunt autem iniquitati ira et indignatio*

but to *those* who from contention and *those* who do

not acquiesce to truth, but believe treachery – anger and indignation;

2:9 *tribulatio et angustia in omnem animam hominis operantis malum Iudaei primum et Graeci*

trouble and anguish, to every human soul doing harm – Jew first, and Greek –

2:10 *gloria autem et honor et pax omni operanti bonum Iudaeo primum et Graeco*

but glory and honor and peace to all doing good – Jew first, and Greek.

God Plays No Favorites
2:11 *non est enim personarum acceptio apud Deum*

For there is no acceptance of persons with God.

2:12 *quicumque enim sine lege peccaverunt sine lege et peribunt et quicumque in lege peccaverunt per legem iudicabuntur*

For whoever has sinned without law will perish without law. And whoever has sinned in law, will be judged through law.

2:13 *non enim auditores legis iusti sunt apud Deum sed factores legis iustificabuntur*

For *the* law's hearers are not fair before God, but *the* law's doers will be justified.

2:14 *cum enim gentes quae legem non habent naturaliter quae legis sunt faciunt eiusmodi legem non habentes ipsi sibi sunt lex*

For when nations who do not have *the* law naturally do what sort of things are in *the* law, they, not having *the* law, are *a* law to themselves –

2:15 *qui ostendunt opus legis scriptum in cordibus suis testimonium reddente illis conscientia ipsorum et inter se invicem cogitationum accusantium aut etiam defendentium*

who show *the* law's work written on their hearts, their conscience returning testimony to them, and their thoughts in turn accusing or even defending,

2:16 *in die cum iudicabit Deus occulta hominum secundum evangelium meum per Iesum Christum*

on *the* day when God will judge humanity's hidden *depths*, according to my good news through Jesus

Christ.

Religious Pride

2:17 *si autem tu Iudaeus cognominaris et requiescis in lege et gloriaris in Deo*

But if you call yourself *a* Jew, and rest in *the* law, and glory in God,

2:18 *et nosti voluntatem et probas utiliora instructus per legem*

and know *the* will, and prove *the* better, instructed by *the* law −

2:19 *confidis te ipsum ducem esse caecorum lumen eorum qui in tenebris sunt*

confident that you yourself are *a* leader of *the* blind, light of those who are in darkness,

2:20 *eruditorem insipientium magistrum infantium habentem formam scientiae et veritatis in lege*

instructor of fools, teacher of infants, having in *the* law *the* form of knowledge and truth −

2:21 *qui ergo alium doces te ipsum non doces qui*

praedicas non furandum furaris

you, therefore, who teach another, do you teach yourself? You who preach, "Don't steal," do you steal?

2:22 *qui dicis non moechandum moecharis qui abominaris idola sacrilegium facis*

You who say, "Don't commit adultery," do you commit adultery? You who detest idols, do you commit sacrilege?

2:23 *qui in lege gloriaris per praevaricationem legis Deum inhonoras*

You who glory in *the* law dishonor God by violating *the* law,

2:24 *nomen enim Dei per vos blasphematur inter gentes sicut scriptum est*

for God's name is blasphemed among nations through you, as is written.[2]

---

[2] Isaiah 52:5: Now therefore, what have I here, saith the LORD, that my people is taken away for nought? they that rule over them make them to howl, saith the LORD; and my name

2:25 *circumcisio quidem prodest si legem observes si autem praevaricator legis sis circumcisio tua praeputium facta est*

Circumcision indeed matters if you keep *the* law. But if you are *a* lawbreaker, your circumcision has become foreskin.

2:26 *si igitur praeputium iustitias legis custodiat nonne praeputium illius in circumcisionem reputabitur*

If therefore *a* foreskinned one keeps *the* law's fairnesses, won't his foreskin be considered as circumcision?

2:27 *et iudicabit quod ex natura est praeputium legem consummans te qui per litteram et circumcisionem praevaricator legis es*

And he that from nature is foreskinned, fulfilling *the* law, will judge you, who through letter and circumcision are *a* lawbreaker.

2:28 *non enim qui in manifesto Iudaeus est neque*

---

continually every day *is* blasphemed.

quae in manifesto in carne circumcisio

For *a* Jew is not one who is conspicuous, nor is circumcision what is conspicuous in flesh,

2:29 *sed qui in abscondito Iudaeus et circumcisio cordis in spiritu non littera cuius laus non ex hominibus sed ex Deo est*

but who *is so* in hidden *things is a* Jew, and circumcision *is* in heart, in spirit not letter, whose praise is not from humans but from God.

What Value Is Jewishness?

Romans 3:1 *quid ergo amplius est Iudaeo aut quae utilitas circumcisionis*

What more, therefore, is *a* Jew, or what *is* circumcision's value?

3:2 *multum per omnem modum primum quidem quia credita sunt illis eloquia Dei*

Much in every manner! First, indeed, because God's words were credited to them.

3:3 *quid enim si quidam illorum non crediderunt numquid incredulitas illorum fidem Dei evacuabit absit*

For what if some of them didn't believe? Their lack of faith doesn't make God's faith void, does it? Far be it!

3:4 *est autem Deus verax omnis autem homo mendax sicut scriptum est ut iustificeris in sermonibus tuis et vincas cum iudicaris*

For God is true, though every man *be a* liar. As is written, "So you may be justified in your words, and triumph when you are judged."[3]

3:5 *si autem iniquitas nostra iustitiam Dei commendat quid dicemus numquid iniquus Deus qui infert iram secundum hominem dico*

"But if our treachery confirms God's fairness, what will we say? Is God who brings wrath treacherous? I am speaking according to man!

3:6 *absit alioquin quomodo iudicabit Deus mundum*

Far be it! Otherwise, how will God judge *the* world?

3:7 *si enim veritas Dei in meo mendacio abundavit in gloriam ipsius quid adhuc et ego tamquam peccator iudicor*

For if God's truth abounded to His glory in my lie, why am I still judged *as a* sinner?

3:8 *et non sicut blasphemamur et sicut aiunt nos quidam dicere faciamus mala ut veniant bona quorum damnatio iusta est*

And why not – as we are slandered and as some say

---

[3] Exact citation unclear.

that we say (whose damnation is fair!) – let us do harm so good may come?

Are We Any Better?

3:9 *quid igitur praecellimus eos nequaquam causati enim sumus Iudaeos et Graecos omnes sub peccato esse*

What, then? Are we better than them? By no means! For we have alleged all Jews and Greeks to be under sin.

3:10 *sicut scriptum est quia non est iustus quisquam*

As is written, "For no one is fair!

3:11 *non est intellegens non est requirens Deum*

"*There* is no intelligent one. *There* is no one seeking God!"

3:12 *omnes declinaverunt simul inutiles facti sunt non est qui faciat bonum non est usque ad unum*

"All have turned aside together. They have become useless. *There* is no one who does good. *There* is not even one!

3:13 *sepulchrum patens est guttur eorum linguis suis dolose agebant venenum aspidum sub labiis eorum*

"Their throat is *an* open grave. They carried on deceptively with their tongues. Asp's venom *is* beneath their lips,

3:14 *quorum os maledictione et amaritudine plenum est*

"whose mouth is full of cursing and bitterness.

3:15 *veloces pedes eorum ad effundendum sanguinem*

"Their feet *are* swift to pouring out blood.

3:16 *contritio et infelicitas in viis eorum*

"Regret and unhappiness *are* in their ways,

3:17 *et viam pacis non cognoverunt*

"and they have not known peace's way.

3:18 *non est timor Dei ante oculos eorum*

"Fear of God is not before their eyes."[4]

Every Mouth Shut

3:19 *scimus autem quoniam quaecumque lex loquitur his qui in lege sunt loquitur ut omne os obstruatur et subditus fiat omnis mundus Deo*

But we know that whatever the law says, it says to those who are in *the* law, so every mouth may be shut and *the* whole world may be subject to God.

3:20 *quia ex operibus legis non iustificabitur omnis caro coram illo per legem enim cognitio peccati*

For no flesh will be justified before Him by works of *the* law, for through law *comes the* recognition of sin.

Fairness Apart From Law

3:21 *nunc autem sine lege iustitia Dei manifestata est testificata a lege et prophetis*

But now God's fairness is made clear apart from *the* law, testified to by *the* law and *the* prophets –

3:22 *iustitia autem Dei per fidem Iesu Christi super omnes qui credunt non enim est distinctio*

---

[4] See Psalm 14:1-3.

God's fairness *comes* through *the* faith of Jesus Christ over all who believe, for there is no distinction.

3:23 *omnes enim peccaverunt et egent gloriam Dei*

For all have sinned and lack God's glory –

3:24 *iustificati gratis per gratiam ipsius per redemptionem quae est in Christo Iesu*

justified freely by His grace, through *the* redemption that is in Christ Jesus,

3:25 *quem proposuit Deus propitiationem per fidem in sanguine ipsius ad ostensionem iustitiae suae propter remissionem praecedentium delictorum*

whom God put forward as atonement through faith in His blood, to *the* demonstration of His fairness, for *the* sake of *the* forgiveness of *the* preceding offenses,

3:26 *in sustentatione Dei ad ostensionem iustitiae eius in hoc tempore ut sit ipse iustus et iustificans eum qui ex fide est Iesu*

in God's endurance, as His fairness's demonstration in this time, so He may be both fair and *the* One making him fair who is of *the* faith of Jesus.

Any Boasting?

3:27 *ubi est ergo gloriatio exclusa est per quam legem factorum non sed per legem fidei*

Where, then, is boasting? It is excluded. By what law? By works? No, but by *the* law of faith.

3:28 *arbitramur enim iustificari hominem per fidem sine operibus legis*

For we consider man to be justified through faith, without *the* law's works.

3:29 *an Iudaeorum Deus tantum nonne et gentium immo et gentium*

Or is He God of Jews only and not of nations? No indeed! Of nations also!

3:30 *quoniam quidem unus Deus qui iustificabit circumcisionem ex fide et praeputium per fidem*

For indeed *there* is one God who will justify *the* circumcision through faith, and *the* foreskinned through faith.

3:31 *legem ergo destruimus per fidem absit sed legem statuimus*

Do we therefore destroy law through faith? Far be it!
But we have established *the* law.

Abraham's Example

4:1 *quid ergo dicemus invenisse Abraham patrem nostrum secundum carnem*

What, then, will we say Abraham, our father according to flesh, found?

4:2 *si enim Abraham ex operibus iustificatus est habet gloriam sed non apud Deum*

For if Abraham was made fair by works, he has glory – though not with God.

4:3 *quid enim scriptura dicit credidit Abraham Deo et reputatum est illi ad iustitiam*

For what does scripture say? "Abraham believed God, and it was reputed to him as fairness."[5]

4:4 *ei autem qui operatur merces non inputatur secundum gratiam sed secundum debitum*

But to one who works, *a* reward is not given according to grace, but according to debt.

---

[5] Genesis 15:6:And he believed in the LORD; and he counted it to him for righteousness.

4:5 *ei vero qui non operatur credenti autem in eum qui iustificat impium reputatur fides eius ad iustitiam*

To him, indeed, who does not work, but believing in Him who makes fair *the* lawless, his faith is considered as fairness.

4:6 *sicut et David dicit beatitudinem hominis cui Deus accepto fert iustitiam sine operibus*

As David also speaks of *the* blessedness of *a* man to whom God, accepting *him*, brings fairness without works.

4:7 *beati quorum remissae sunt iniquitates et quorum tecta sunt peccata*

"Blessed *are* those whose treacheries are forgiven and whose sins are covered.

4:8 *beatus vir cui non inputabit Dominus peccatum*

"*A* man *is* blessed whom *the* Lord will not charge with sin."[6]

4:9 *beatitudo ergo haec in circumcisione an etiam in*

---

[6] See Psalm 32:12.

praeputio dicimus enim quia reputata est Abrahae fides ad iustitiam

Is this blessedness, then, *only* in circumcision, or even in foreskin? For we say that Abraham's faith was reputed as fairness.

4:10 *quomodo ergo reputata est in circumcisione an in praeputio non in circumcisione sed in praeputio*

How, then, was it reputed? In circumcision or in foreskin? Not in circumcision, but in foreskin![7]

4:11 *et signum accepit circumcisionis signaculum iustitiae fidei quae est in praeputio ut sit pater omnium credentium per praeputium ut reputetur et illis ad iustitiam*

And he received the sign of circumcision *as a* seal of *the* fairness of faith, which is in foreskin, so he may be father of all believing through foreskin, so it may be reputed also to them as fairness;

4:12 *et sit pater circumcisionis non his tantum qui*

---

[7] Abraham believed God's promise before he was circumcised. Circumcision followed faith, as a sign of obedience rather than a cause of salvation.

*sunt ex circumcisione sed et his qui sectantur vestigia
quae est in praeputio fidei patris nostri Abrahae*

and that he may be circumcision's father, not only of
those who are of circumcision, but also of those who
follow *the* footsteps, which is *the* faith of our father
Abraham *while* in foreskin.

4:13 *non enim per legem promissio Abrahae aut
semini eius ut heres esset mundi sed per iustitiam
fidei*

For Abraham's promise is not through *the* law, or his
seed's, that he might be *the* world's heir – but through
faith's fairness.

4:14 *si enim qui ex lege heredes sunt exinanita est
fides abolita est promissio*

For if *the* heirs are from law, faith is emptied and *the*
promise is abolished.

4:15 *lex enim iram operatur ubi enim non est lex nec
praevaricatio*

For law works anger. For where law is not, neither *is
there* lawbreaking.

4:16 *ideo ex fide ut secundum gratiam ut firma sit promissio omni semini non ei qui ex lege est solum sed et ei qui ex fide est Abrahae qui est pater omnium nostrum*

Therefore, *the promise is* from faith, that his seed's promise may be established according to grace – not to him who is of *the* law only, but also to him who is of Abraham's faith, who is father of all of us.

4:17 *sicut scriptum est quia patrem multarum gentium posui te ante Deum cui credidit qui vivificat mortuos et vocat quae non sunt tamquam ea quae sunt*

As is written, "For I appointed you as father of many nations,"[8] before God, whom he believed – that He can revive *the* dead, and call *possibilities* that are not as if they are –

4:18 *qui contra spem in spem credidit ut fieret pater multarum gentium secundum quod dictum est sic erit semen tuum*

who, against hope, believed in hope that he might be father of many nations, according to what was said:

---

[8] See Genesis 17:4-5.

"So your seed will be."[9]

4:19 *et non infirmatus fide consideravit corpus suum emortuum cum fere centum annorum esset et emortuam vulvam Sarrae*

And not weak in faith, he considered his body dead – when he was almost a hundred years old, and Sarah's vulva dead.

4:20 *in repromissione etiam Dei non haesitavit diffidentia sed confortatus est fide dans gloriam Deo*

And he did not hesitate, distrusting God's guarantee, but was strengthened by faith, giving glory to God,

4:21 *plenissime sciens quia quaecumque promisit potens est et facere*

knowing full well that whatever He promised, He is mighty also to do.

4:22 *ideo et reputatum est illi ad iustitiam*

Therefore, it was reputed also to him as fairness.

---

[9] See Genesis 15:5.

4:23 *non est autem scriptum tantum propter ipsum quia reputatum est illi*

But it was not written only on his behalf, that it was reputed to him,

4:24 *sed et propter nos quibus reputabitur credentibus in eum qui suscitavit Iesum Dominum nostrum a mortuis*

but also on our behalf, to whom *fairness* will be reputed – to those believing in Him who raised up Jesus our Lord from *the* dead,

4:25 *qui traditus est propter delicta nostra et resurrexit propter iustificationem nostram*

who was handed over for our offenses, and raised up for our justification.

Justified From Faith

Romans 5:1 *iustificati igitur ex fide pacem habeamus ad Deum per Dominum nostrum Iesum Christum*

Justified, therefore, from faith, may we have peace toward God, through our Lord Jesus Christ –

5:2 *per quem et accessum habemus fide in gratiam istam in qua stamus et gloriamur in spe gloriae filiorum Dei*

through whom we have access in His grace by faith, in which we are standing. And we glory in *the* hope of God's children's glory.

5:3 *non solum autem sed et gloriamur in tribulationibus scientes quod tribulatio patientiam operatur*

Not only that, but we also glory in troubles, knowing that trouble works patience,

5:4 *patientia autem probationem probatio vero spem*

but patience proving, and proving hope.

5:5 *spes autem non confundit quia caritas Dei*

diffusa est in cordibus nostris per Spiritum Sanctum
qui datus est nobis

But hope does not confound, because God's affection
is spread through our hearts through *the* Holy Spirit,
who is given to us.

5:6 *ut quid enim Christus cum adhuc infirmi essemus*
secundum tempus pro impiis mortuus est

For Christ, when we were still weak, according to *the*
time, died for *the* lawless –

5:7 *vix enim pro iusto quis moritur nam pro bono*
forsitan quis et audeat mori

for one hardly dies for *the* fair (though someone
might dare to die also for *the* good)!

5:8 *commendat autem suam caritatem Deus in nos*
quoniam cum adhuc peccatores essemus

But God commends His affection in us that, when we
were still sinners,

5:9 *Christus pro nobis mortuus est multo igitur*
magis iustificati nunc in sanguine ipsius salvi erimus
ab ira per ipsum

Christ died for us. Much more, therefore, now made fair in His blood, will we be made safe from anger through Him.

If, When We Were Enemies

5:10 *si enim cum inimici essemus reconciliati sumus Deo per mortem Filii eius multo magis reconciliati salvi erimus in vita ipsius*

For if, when we were enemies, we were reconciled to God through His Son's death, much more, *now* reconciled, will we be made secure in His life.

5:11 *non solum autem sed et gloriamur in Deo per Dominum nostrum Iesum Christum per quem nunc reconciliationem accepimus*

Not only that, but we also glory in God through our Lord Jesus Christ, through whom we have now received reconciliation.

5:12 *propterea sicut per unum hominem in hunc mundum peccatum intravit et per peccatum mors et ita in omnes homines mors pertransiit in quo omnes peccaverunt*

Because, as through one man sin entered into this world, and death through sin, so also death has passed through to all humans, in that all have sinned.

5:13 *usque ad legem enim peccatum erat in mundo peccatum autem non inputatur cum lex non est*

For sin was in *the* world even to *the* law, but sin is not counted up where law is not.

5:14 *sed regnavit mors ab Adam usque ad Mosen etiam in eos qui non peccaverunt in similitudinem praevaricationis Adae qui est forma futuri*

But death reigned from Adam even to Moses, even in those who had not sinned in *the* likeness of Adam's lawbreaking – who is *the* future's form.

5:15 *sed non sicut delictum ita et donum si enim unius delicto multi mortui sunt multo magis gratia Dei et donum in gratiam unius hominis Iesu Christi in plures abundavit*

But not like *the* offense, so also *the* gift! For if by one offense many died, God's grace and *the* gift in grace by one man, Jesus Christ, abounded much more to many.

5:16 *et non sicut per unum peccantem ita et donum nam iudicium ex uno in condemnationem gratia* *autem ex multis delictis in iustificationem*

And not as through one sin, so also *the* gift! For judgment came from one into condemnation, but grace *comes* from many offenses into justification.

5:17 *si enim in unius delicto mors regnavit per unum multo magis abundantiam gratiae et donationis et iustitiae accipientes in vita regnabunt per unum Iesum Christum*

For if death reigned in one offense through one, *those* receiving grace's abundance and gifts and fairnesses will reign much more through one, Jesus Christ.

5:18 *igitur sicut per unius delictum in omnes homines in condemnationem sic et per unius iustitiam in omnes homines in iustificationem vitae*

Therefore, as through one offense all men *came* to condemnation, so also through one *act of* fairness all men *will come* to life's justification.

5:19 *sicut enim per inoboedientiam unius hominis peccatores constituti sunt multi ita et per unius oboeditionem iusti constituentur multi*

For as through one man's disobedience many were

constituted as sinners, so also through one's obedience, many will be constituted as fair.

5:20 *lex autem subintravit ut abundaret delictum ubi autem abundavit delictum superabundavit gratia*

But law entered in secretly, that offense might abound. But where offense abounded, grace abounded even more –

5:21 *ut sicut regnavit peccatum in morte ita et gratia regnet per iustitiam in vitam aeternam per Iesum Christum Dominum nostrum*

that, as sin reigned in death, so also grace may reign through fairness into eternal life, through Jesus Christ our Lord.

Sin or Grace

Romans 6:1 *quid ergo dicemus permanebimus in peccato ut gratia abundet*

What, then will we say? Will we remain in sin so grace may abound?

6:2 *absit qui enim mortui sumus peccato quomodo adhuc vivemus in illo*

Far be it! For we have died to sin – how will we still live in it?

6:3 *an ignoratis quia quicumque baptizati sumus in Christo Iesu in morte ipsius baptizati sumus*

Or do you not know that whoever we *are who* are baptized into Christ Jesus, we are baptized into His death?

6:4 *consepulti enim sumus cum illo per baptismum in mortem ut quomodo surrexit Christus a mortuis per gloriam Patris ita et nos in novitate vitae ambulemus*

For we are buried together with him through baptism into death, that, as Christ rose from *the* dead through *the* Father's glory, so we also may walk in life's newness.

6:5 *si enim conplantati facti sumus similitudini mortis eius simul et resurrectionis erimus*

For if we have been planted with Him in His death's likeness, we will also be resurrected at the same time,

6:6 *hoc scientes quia vetus homo noster simul crucifixus est ut destruatur corpus peccati ut ultra non serviamus peccato*

knowing this: that our old man was crucified at once, that sin's body may be destroyed, so we may no longer serve sin –

6:7 *qui enim mortuus est iustificatus est a peccato*

for *one* who has died is justified from sin.

If We Have Died

6:8 *si autem mortui sumus cum Christo credimus quia simul etiam vivemus cum Christo*

But if we have died with Christ, we believe also that we will even live with Christ,

6:9 *scientes quod Christus surgens ex mortuis iam non moritur mors illi ultra non dominabitur*

knowing that Christ, rising from *the* dead, no longer
may die. Death will dominate Him no further.

6:10 *quod enim mortuus est peccato mortuus est
semel quod autem vivit vivit Deo*

For that He died, He died once to sin; but that He
lives, He lives to God.

6:11 *ita et vos existimate vos mortuos quidem esse
peccato viventes autem Deo in Christo Iesu*

So you also consider yourselves to be dead indeed to
sin, but living to God in Christ Jesus.

Do Not Let Sin
6:12 *non ergo regnet peccatum in vestro mortali
corpore ut oboediatis concupiscentiis eius*

Therefore, do not let sin reign in your mortal body, so
you obey its lusts.

6:13 *sed neque exhibeatis membra vestra arma
iniquitatis peccato sed exhibete vos Deo tamquam ex
mortuis viventes et membra vestra arma iustitiae Deo*

Yet neither ought you present your members *as*
treachery's weapons to sin, but present yourselves to

God, as if living from *the* dead, and your members *as* fairness's weapons to God.

6:14 *peccatum enim vobis non dominabitur non enim sub lege estis sed sub gratia*

For sin will not dominate you, for you are not under law, but under grace.

6:15 *quid ergo peccavimus quoniam non sumus sub lege sed sub gratia absit*

What, then? Have we sinned because we are not under law but under grace? Far be it!

Whose Slave Are You?
6:16 *nescitis quoniam cui exhibetis vos servos ad oboediendum servi estis eius cui oboeditis sive peccati sive oboeditionis ad iustitiam*

Do you not know that you show yourselves as slaves to whomever you obey? You are his slaves whom you obey – whether of sin, *or* of obedience to fairness.

6:17 *gratias autem Deo quod fuistis servi peccati oboedistis autem ex corde in eam formam doctrinae in qua traditi estis*

But thanks *be* to God that *though* you were sin's slaves, you have obeyed from *the* heart in that form of teaching to which you were handed over.

6:18 *liberati autem a peccato servi facti estis iustitiae*

But, freed from sin, you have become fairness's slaves.

6:19 *humanum dico propter infirmitatem carnis vestrae sicut enim exhibuistis membra vestra servire inmunditiae et iniquitati ad iniquitatem ita nunc exhibete membra vestra servire iustitiae in sanctificationem*

I am speaking *as a* human, because of your flesh's weakness. For as you presented your members to serve uncleanness and treachery, toward treachery, so now present your members to serve fairness toward being made holy.

When You Were Sin's Slaves
6:20 *cum enim servi essetis peccati liberi fuistis iustitiae*

For when you were sin's slaves, you were free from fairness.

6:21 *quem ergo fructum habuistis tunc in quibus nunc erubescitis nam finis illorum mors est*

What fruit, therefore, did you have then, of which now you are ashamed – for death is their end!

6:22 *nunc vero liberati a peccato servi autem facti Deo habetis fructum vestrum in sanctificationem finem vero vitam aeternam*

Now, though, freed from sin but made slaves to God, you have your fruit toward being made holy – indeed *a* destination of eternal life.

6:23 *stipendia enim peccati mors gratia autem Dei vita aeterna in Christo Iesu Domino nostro*

For sin's stipend *is* death, but God's grace *is* eternal life in Christ Jesus our Lord.

Law Rules During Natural Life

Romans 7:1 *an ignoratis fratres scientibus enim legem loquor quia lex in homine dominatur quanto tempore vivit*

Or do you not know, brothers – for I am speaking to those knowing *the* law – that *the* law rules in *a* man for as long as he lives?

7:2 *nam quae sub viro est mulier vivente viro alligata est legi si autem mortuus fuerit vir soluta est a lege viri*

For *a* woman who is under *a* man is bound by law, *the* man living. But if *the* man dies, she is released from *the* man by law.

7:3 *igitur vivente viro vocabitur adultera si fuerit cum alio viro si autem mortuus fuerit vir eius liberata est a lege ut non sit adultera si fuerit cum alio viro*

Therefore, *while the* man *is* living, she will be called *an* adulterer if she is with another man. But if her husband dies, she is freed from *the* law, so she may not be *an* adulterer if she is with another man.

7:4 *itaque fratres mei et vos mortificati estis legi per corpus Christi ut sitis alterius qui ex mortuis* *resurrexit ut fructificaremus Deo*

And therefore, my brothers, you also have died to *the* law through Christ's body, so you may be another's who has risen from *the* dead – so you may bear fruit to God.

When We Were in Flesh

7:5 *cum enim essemus in carne passiones peccatorum quae per legem erant operabantur in membris nostris ut fructificarent morti*

For when we were in flesh, sin's passions, which were through *the* law, worked in our members so we could bear fruit to death.

7:6 *nunc autem soluti sumus a lege morientes in quo detinebamur ita ut serviamus in novitate spiritus et non in vetustate litterae*

Now, though, we are released from *the* law, dying to that which held us prisoner, so we may serve in spirit's newness and not in *the* letter's oldness.

7:7 *quid ergo dicemus lex peccatum est absit sed peccatum non cognovi nisi per legem nam concupiscentiam nesciebam nisi lex diceret non concupisces*

What will we say then? *The* law is sin? Far be it! But I did not know sin except through law. For I hadn't known lusting, except *the* law had said "You will not lust!"[10]

7:8 *occasione autem accepta peccatum per mandatum operatum est in me omnem concupiscentiam sine lege enim peccatum mortuum erat*

But sin, receiving opportunity through *the* commandment, worked every lust in me. For without law, sin was dead.

7:9 *ego autem vivebam sine lege aliquando sed cum venisset mandatum peccatum revixit*

But I lived some time without *the* law. Yet when *the* commandment had come, sin revived –

7:10 *ego autem mortuus sum et inventum est mihi mandatum quod erat ad vitam hoc esse ad mortem*

but I died. And this commandment, which was to life, was found in me to be to death.

---

[10] The reference is to the Tenth Commandment. See Exodus 20:17; Deuteronomy 5:21.

7:11 *nam peccatum occasione accepta per mandatum seduxit me et per illud occidit*

For sin, receiving opportunity through *the* commandment, seduced and killed me through it.

7:12 *itaque lex quidem sancta et mandatum sanctum et iustum et bonum*

So *the* law indeed is holy, and *the* commandment holy and fair and good.

7:13 *quod ergo bonum est mihi factum est mors absit sed peccatum ut appareat peccatum per bonum mihi operatum est mortem ut fiat supra modum peccans peccatum per mandatum*

Did therefore, what is good become death to me? Far be it! But sin, that it may appear *as* sin, *was* working death to me through *the* good, that sin may become sin beyond measure through *the* commandment.

Sold Under Sin

7:14 *scimus enim quod lex spiritalis est ego autem carnalis sum venundatus sub peccato*

For we know that *the* law is spiritual. But I am fleshly, sold under sin.

7:15 *quod enim operor non intellego non enim quod volo hoc ago sed quod odi illud facio*

For I do not understand what I am doing. For this *act* I am doing I do not want. But what I hated, that I am doing.

7:16 *si autem quod nolo illud facio consentio legi quoniam bona*

But if I am doing that which I do not want, I agree about *the* law that *it is* good.

7:17 *nunc autem iam non ego operor illud sed quod habitat in me peccatum*

But already now I am not doing it, but sin that is living in me.

7:18 *scio enim quia non habitat in me hoc est in carne mea bonum nam velle adiacet mihi perficere autem bonum non invenio*

For I know that good does not live in me – that is, in my flesh. For to will lies near, but to complete *the* good I do not find.

7:19 *non enim quod volo bonum hoc facio sed quod*

nolo malum hoc ago

For *the* good that I want, this I do not do. But *the* harm that I do not want, this I do.

7:20 *si autem quod nolo illud facio non ego operor illud sed quod habitat in me peccatum*

But if I do what I do not want, I am not working it, but sin which lives in me.

7:21 *invenio igitur legem volenti mihi facere bonum quoniam mihi malum adiacet*

I find, therefore, *a* law that, wanting to do *the* good, harm lies near me.

7:22 *condelector enim legi Dei secundum interiorem hominem*

For I am delighted in God's law, according to *the* inner man.

7:23 *video autem aliam legem in membris meis repugnantem legi mentis meae et captivantem me in lege peccati quae est in membris meis*

But I see another law in my members, fighting against

my mind's law, and capturing me in sin's law – which is in my members.

7:24 *infelix ego homo quis me liberabit de corpore mortis huius*

I *am an* unhappy man! Who will free me from this body of death?

7:25 *gratia Dei per Iesum Christum Dominum nostrum igitur ego ipse mente servio legi Dei carne autem legi peccati*

God's grace *will*, through Jesus Christ our Lord! Therefore, I myself serve God's law in mind, but sin's law in flesh.

No Damnation

Romans 8:1 *nihil ergo nunc damnationis est his qui sunt in Christo Iesu qui non secundum carnem ambulant*

Now, then, *there* is no damnation to those who are in Christ Jesus, who are not walking according to flesh.

8:2 *lex enim Spiritus vitae in Christo Iesu liberavit me a lege peccati et mortis*

For *the* law of life's Spirit in Christ Jesus has freed me from *the* law of sin and death.

8:3 *nam quod inpossibile erat legis in quo infirmabatur per carnem Deus Filium suum mittens in similitudinem carnis peccati et de peccato damnavit peccatum in carne*

For what was impossible for law, in that it was weakened through flesh, God, sending His Son in *the* likeness of sin's flesh and from sin, damned sin in *the* flesh,

8:4 *ut iustificatio legis impleretur in nobis qui non secundum carnem ambulamus sed secundum Spiritum*

that law's justification might be fulfilled in us, who

walk not according to flesh but according to Spirit.

Living According to Spirit

8:5 *qui enim secundum carnem sunt quae carnis sunt sapiunt qui vero secundum Spiritum quae sunt Spiritus sentiunt*

For *those* who are *living* according to flesh taste what *things* are of flesh.   Yet *those* who are *living* according to Spirit, feel what *things* are of Spirit.

8:6 *nam prudentia carnis mors prudentia autem Spiritus vita et pax*

For flesh's prudence *is* death, but Spirit's prudence *is* life and peace,

8:7 *quoniam sapientia carnis inimicitia est in Deum legi enim Dei non subicitur nec enim potest*

because flesh's wisdom is enmity against God. For it is not subject to God's law, nor can it *be*.

8:8 *qui autem in carne sunt Deo placere non possunt*

But *those* who are in flesh cannot please God.

8:9 *vos autem in carne non estis sed in Spiritu si*

tamen Spiritus Dei habitat in vobis si quis autem Spiritum Christi non habet hic non est eius

But you are not in flesh, but in Spirit – if God's Spirit still lives among you. But if someone does not have Christ's Spirit, he is not His.

8:10 *si autem Christus in vobis est corpus quidem mortuum est propter peccatum spiritus vero vita propter iustificationem*

But if Christ is among you, *the* body indeed is dead because of sin, yet *the* spirit alive because of justification –

8:11 *quod si Spiritus eius qui suscitavit Iesum a mortuis habitat in vobis qui suscitavit Iesum Christum a mortuis vivificabit et mortalia corpora vestra propter inhabitantem Spiritum eius in vobis*

that if His Spirit who raised Jesus from *the* dead lives among you, *the One* who raised Jesus Christ from *the* dead will give life to your mortal bodies also, because of His Spirit living among you.

We Are Debtors
8:12 *ergo fratres debitores sumus non carni ut secundum carnem vivamus*

Therefore, brothers, we are debtors – not to flesh, so
we can live according to flesh,

8:13 *si enim secundum carnem vixeritis moriemini si
autem Spiritu facta carnis mortificatis vivetis*

for if you live according to flesh, you will die. But if
by Spirit, flesh's acts destroyed, you will live.

8:14 *quicumque enim Spiritu Dei aguntur hii filii
sunt Dei*

For whoever live by God's Spirit, these are God's
children.

Abba, Father

8:15 *non enim accepistis spiritum servitutis iterum in
timore sed accepistis Spiritum adoptionis filiorum in
quo clamamus Abba Pater*

For you have not received slavery's spirit again in
fear, but you have received adoption's Spirit as
children, in which we cry out, "Abba, Father!"

8:16 *ipse Spiritus testimonium reddit spiritui nostro
quod sumus filii Dei*

The same Spirit bears witness to our spirit that we are

God's children.

8:17 *si autem filii et heredes heredes quidem Dei coheredes autem Christi si tamen conpatimur ut et conglorificemur*

But if children, also heirs – indeed, God's heirs, but Christ's co-heirs – if still we suffer together, that we also may be glorified together.

Not Worth Comparing
8:18 *existimo enim quod non sunt condignae passiones huius temporis ad futuram gloriam quae revelabitur in nobis*

For I consider that this season's sufferings are not worth comparing to glory's future, which will be revealed among us.

8:19 *nam expectatio creaturae revelationem filiorum Dei expectat*

For *the* created order's expectation awaits *the* revelation of God's children.

8:20 *vanitati enim creatura subiecta est non volens sed propter eum qui subiecit in spem*

For *the* created order is subjected to futility, not willingly, but because of Him who subjected *it* in hope –

8:21 *quia et ipsa creatura liberabitur a servitute corruptionis in libertatem gloriae filiorum Dei*

for *the* same created order will be freed from corruption's slavery – into *the* freedom of God's children's glory.

The Created Order Groans
8:22 *scimus enim quod omnis creatura ingemescit et parturit usque adhuc*

For we know that *the* whole created order groans and suffers even to *the* present –

8:23 *non solum autem illa sed et nos ipsi primitias Spiritus habentes et ipsi intra nos gemimus adoptionem filiorum expectantes redemptionem corporis nostri*

but not only them, yet we ourselves also, having *the* Spirit's first fruits. And we also are groaning within ourselves, awaiting adoption as children, *the* buying back of our bodies.

8:24 *spe enim salvi facti sumus spes autem quae videtur non est spes nam quod videt quis quid sperat*

For we are made secure in hope. But hope which is seen is not hope, for who hopes for what he sees?

8:25 *si autem quod non videmus speramus per patientiam expectamus*

But if we hope for what we do not see, we wait with patience.

Spirit Prays

8:26 *similiter autem et Spiritus adiuvat infirmitatem nostram nam quid oremus sicut oportet nescimus sed ipse Spiritus postulat pro nobis gemitibus inenarrabilibus*

But Spirit likewise also helps our weakness. For what we may pray, as is fitting, we do not know. Yet *the* Spirit Himself prays for us, with unutterable sighs.

8:27 *qui autem scrutatur corda scit quid desideret Spiritus quia secundum Deum postulat pro sanctis*

But *One* who examines hearts knows what *the* Spirit desires, because He pleads according to God for *the* holy *ones*.

8:28 *scimus autem quoniam diligentibus Deum omnia cooperantur in bonum his qui secundum propositum vocati sunt sancti*

But we know that to those delighting in God all *things* work together to good, to those who, according to *the* proposition, are called holy.

8:29 *nam quos praescivit et praedestinavit conformes fieri imaginis Filii eius ut sit ipse primogenitus in multis fratribus*

For *those* whom He knew in advance, He also destined in advance to be conformed to His Son's image – so He may be firstborn among many brothers.

8:30 *quos autem praedestinavit hos et vocavit et quos vocavit hos et iustificavit quos autem iustificavit illos et glorificavit*

But *those* whom He destined in advance, He also called. And *those* whom He called, He also justified. But those whom He justified, He also glorified.

Who Can Be Against Us?

8:31 *quid ergo dicemus ad haec si Deus pro nobis quis contra nos*

What, therefore, will we say to this? If God *is* for us, who *is* against us?

8:32 *qui etiam Filio suo non pepercit sed pro nobis omnibus tradidit illum quomodo non etiam cum illo omnia nobis donabit*

One who has not spared even His Son, yet handed Him over for all of us – how will He not also give us all *things* with Him?

8:33 *quis accusabit adversus electos Dei Deus qui iustificat*

Who will make *an* accusation against God's chosen *ones*? *Will* God, who justifies?

8:34 *quis est qui condemnet Christus Iesus qui mortuus est immo qui resurrexit qui et est ad dexteram Dei qui etiam interpellat pro nobis*

Who exists who will condemn? *Will* Christ Jesus, who has died – more correctly, who has risen, who is at God's right hand, who even intercedes on our behalf?

8:35 *quis nos separabit a caritate Christi tribulatio an angustia an persecutio an fames an nuditas an* *periculum an gladius*

Who will separate us from Christ's favor? *Will* anguish, or persecution, or hunger, or nakedness, or danger, or sword?

8:36 *sicut scriptum est quia propter te mortificamur tota die aestimati sumus ut oves occisionis*

As is written, "For because of you, we are dying all day. We are considered as sheep for slaughter."[11]

We Are Overcoming
8:37 *sed in his omnibus superamus propter eum qui dilexit nos*

Yet in all these *events* we are overcoming, because of Him who has delighted in us.

8:38 *certus sum enim quia neque mors neque vita neque angeli neque principatus neque instantia neque futura neque fortitudines*

For I am certain that neither death, nor life, nor angels, nor rulers, nor present, nor future, nor strengths,

---

[11] See Psalm 44:22.

8:39 *neque altitudo neque profundum neque creatura alia poterit nos separare a caritate Dei quae est in Christo Iesu Domino nostro*

nor height, nor depth, nor *any* other created order can separate us from God's favor, which is in Christ Jesus our Lord.

Sadness Over Israel

Romans 9:1 *veritatem dico in Christo non mentior testimonium mihi perhibente conscientia mea in Spiritu Sancto*

I speak truth in Christ – I do not lie – my conscience bearing witness to me in Holy Spirit,

9:2 *quoniam tristitia est mihi magna et continuus dolor cordi meo*

that great sadness is mine, and continuing pain in my heart.

9:3 *optabam enim ipse ego anathema esse a Christo pro fratribus meis qui sunt cognati mei secundum carnem*

For I wish I myself were cursed from Christ for my brothers' sake, who are my kinsmen according to flesh –

9:4 *qui sunt Israhelitae quorum adoptio est filiorum et gloria et testamenta et legislatio et obsequium et promissa*

who are Israelites, whose is adoption *as* children, and *whose are* glory, and covenant, and law, and prayer, and promise –

9:5 *quorum patres et ex quibus Christus secundum carnem qui est super omnia Deus benedictus in saecula amen*

whose are *the* fathers, and from whom *is* Christ according to flesh – who is God over all, blessed in *the* age. Amen.

Has God's Word Failed?

9:6 *non autem quod exciderit verbum Dei non enim omnes qui ex Israhel hii sunt Israhel*

But *it is* not that God's word failed, for not all who are from Israel are Israel,[12]

9:7 *neque quia semen sunt Abrahae omnes filii sed in Isaac vocabitur tibi semen*

nor are all *the* children Abraham's seed. But "Seed will be called to you in Isaac"[13] –

9:8 *id est non qui filii carnis hii filii Dei sed qui filii*

---

[12] See Exodus 12:38.

[13] See Genesis 21:12.

sunt promissionis aestimantur in semine

that is, God's children are not those who are children by flesh. Yet those who are children by promise are esteemed as seed.

9:9 *promissionis enim verbum hoc est secundum hoc tempus veniam et erit Sarrae filius*

For *the* word's promise is this: "According to this time, I will come, and *a* son will be to Sarah."[14]

9:10 *non solum autem sed et Rebecca ex uno concubitum habens Isaac patre nostro*

Not only that, but also Rebecca, having *conceived* from one sexual act with Isaac our father,

9:11 *cum enim nondum nati fuissent aut aliquid egissent bonum aut malum ut secundum electionem propositum Dei maneret*

when still they had not been born or done anything either good or harmful, that election's purpose might remain according to God –

---

[14] See Genesis 18:14.

9:12 *non ex operibus sed ex vocante dictum est ei quia maior serviet minori*

not from work, but from calling – it was said to her that *"The* older will serve the younger."[15]

9:13 *sicut scriptum est Iacob dilexi Esau autem odio habui*

As is written, "I delighted in Jacob, but had hatred for Esau."[16]

Is God Unfair?
9:14 *quid ergo dicemus numquid iniquitas apud Deum absit*

What, then, will we say? There isn't treachery with God, is there? Far be it!

9:15 *Mosi enim dicit miserebor cuius misereor et misericordiam praestabo cuius miserebor*

For He says to Moses, "I will pity whom I pity, and

---

[15] See Genesis 25:22-23.

[16] Citation unknown.

lend mercy to whom I have mercy."[17]

9:16 *igitur non volentis neque currentis sed miserentis Dei*

Therefore, *it is* not by willing, nor by efforts, but by God's mercy.

9:17 *dicit enim scriptura Pharaoni quia in hoc ipsum excitavi te ut ostendam in te virtutem meam et ut adnuntietur nomen meum in universa terra*

For scripture says of Pharaoh that, "I have raised you up in this thing, that I may show My power in you, and that My name may be told in all *the* land."[18]

9:18 *ergo cuius vult miseretur et quem vult indurat*

Therefore, He will have mercy on whom He chooses, and harden whom He chooses.

Who Resists His Will?

9:19 *dicis itaque mihi quid adhuc queritur voluntati enim eius quis resistit*

---

[17] See Exodus 33:19.

[18] See Exodus 10:1-2.

So you will say to me, "What still is *the* complaint, for who resists His will?"

9:20 *o homo tu quis es qui respondeas Deo numquid dicit figmentum ei qui se finxit quid me fecisti sic*

O man, who are you who responds to God? *The* thing formed won't say to *the One* who formed it, 'Why did you make me so,' will it?

9:21 *an non habet potestatem figulus luti ex eadem massa facere aliud quidem vas in honorem aliud vero in contumeliam*

Or, doesn't *the* potter have power to make from *the* same lump of clay one vessel indeed for dignified *uses* and another, truly, for undignified *ones*?

The Riddle of God's Patience
9:22 *quod si volens Deus ostendere iram et notam facere potentiam suam sustinuit in multa patientia vasa irae aptata in interitum*

What if God, wanting to show wrath and make known His power, put up with wrath's vessels with much patience, *vessels* formed for destruction –

9:23 *ut ostenderet divitias gloriae suae in vasa*

misericordiae quae praeparavit in gloriam

so He could show His glory's riches to mercy's vessels, which He has prepared in glory –

9:24 *quos et vocavit nos non solum ex Iudaeis sed etiam ex gentibus*

us whom He also called, not only from Jews, but even from *the* nations?

9:25 *sicut in Osee dicit vocabo non plebem meam plebem meam et non misericordiam consecutam misericordiam consecutam*

As He says in Hosea, "I will call 'Not My People' 'My People,' and 'Not Obtaining Mercy' 'Obtaining Mercy.'"[19]

9:26 *et erit in loco ubi dictum est eis non plebs mea vos ibi vocabuntur filii Dei vivi*

"And it will be in *the* place where it was said to them, "You are not My people," they will be called there

---

[19] See Hosea 2:23.

"*The* Living God's children."[20]

Israel's Remnant

9:27 *Esaias autem clamat pro Israhel si fuerit numerus filiorum Israhel tamquam harena maris reliquiae salvae fient*

But Isaiah cries out for Israel, "If *the* number of Israel's children was like *the* sea's sand, *a* remnant will be secured."[21]

9:28 *verbum enim consummans et brevians in aequitate quia verbum breviatum faciet Dominus super terram*

For *the* word is consuming and cutting short in equity, because *the* Lord will make *the* word cut short over *the* land.

9:29 *et sicut praedixit Esaias nisi Dominus Sabaoth reliquisset nobis semen sicut Sodoma facti essemus et sicut Gomorra similes fuissemus*

And, as Isaiah said before, "If Lord Sabaoth had not

---

[20] See Hosea 2:24.

[21] See Isaiah 10:22.

left us seed, we would have become like Sodom, and have been like Gomorrah."[22]

Who Found Fairness?

9:30 *quid ergo dicemus quod gentes quae non sectabantur iustitiam adprehenderunt iustitiam iustitiam autem quae ex fide est*

What, then, will we say? That nations which did not seek fairness have grasped fairness, but *a* fairness that is from faith –

9:31 *Israhel vero sectans legem iustitiae in legem iustitiae non pervenit*

yet Israel, seeking fairness's law, has not found fairness in *the* law?

9:32 *quare quia non ex fide sed quasi ex operibus offenderunt in lapidem offensionis*

Why? Because they sought not from faith, but as if from works. They have struck against *the* stone of displeasure.

9:33 *sicut scriptum est ecce pono in Sion lapidem*

---

[22] See Isaiah 1:9.

offensionis et petram scandali et omnis qui credit in eum non confundetur

As is written, "Look, I place *a* stone of displeasure in Sion, and *a* rock of stumbling, and everyone who believes in Him will not be confounded."[23]

---

[23] See Isaiah 28:16.

My Heart's Will

Romans 10:1 *fratres voluntas quidem cordis mei et obsecratio ad Deum fit pro illis in salutem*

Brothers, may my heart's will, indeed, and prayer to God be on their behalf, to security!

10:2 *testimonium enim perhibeo illis quod aemulationem Dei habent sed non secundum scientiam*

For I bear them witness that they have *an* envy for God, yet not according to knowledge.

10:3 *ignorantes enim Dei iustitiam et suam quaerentes statuere iustitiae Dei non sunt subiecti*

For, not knowing God's fairness and seeking to set up their own, they have not submitted to God's fairness.

Christ Is the Law's Purpose

10:4 *finis enim legis Christus ad iustitiam omni credenti*

For Christ *is the* law's purpose to fairness for all *those* believing.

10:5 *Moses enim scripsit quoniam iustitiam quae ex*

lege est qui fecerit homo vivet in ea

For Moses wrote that "*A* man who works *the* fairness that is from law will live in it."[24]

10:6 *quae autem ex fide est iustitia sic dicit ne dixeris in corde tuo quis ascendit in caelum id est Christum deducere*

But *the* fairness that is from faith speaks this way: "Do not say in your heart, 'Who climbs into *the* sky?' – that is, to bring Christ down –* [25]

10:7 *aut quis descendit in abyssum hoc est Christum ex mortuis revocare*

"or, 'Who climbs down into *the* abyss?'" – this is, to call Christ back from *the* dead.[26]

Words of Salvation
10:8 *sed quid dicit prope est verbum in ore tuo et in corde tuo hoc est verbum fidei quod praedicamus*

---

[24] See Leviticus 18:5.

[25] See Deuteronomy 30:12.

[26] See Deuteronomy 30:13.

But what does it say? *"The* word is near, in your mouth and in your heart" – that is, faith's word which we are preaching – [27]

10:9 *quia si confitearis in ore tuo Dominum Iesum et in corde tuo credideris quod Deus illum excitavit ex mortuis salvus eris*

that if you confess *the* Lord Jesus with your mouth, and believe in your heart that God raised Him from *the* dead, you will be made secure.

10:10 *corde enim creditur ad iustitiam ore autem confessio fit in salutem*

For *the Word* is believed by *the* heart to fairness, but confession is made by *the* mouth to security.

10:11 *dicit enim scriptura omnis qui credit in illum non confundetur*

For scripture says, "Everyone who believes in Him will not be confounded."[28]

---

[27] See Deuteronomy 30:14.

[28] See Isaiah 28:16.

10:12 *non enim est distinctio Iudaei et Graeci nam idem Dominus omnium dives in omnes qui invocant illum*

For there is no distinction between Jew and Greek. For *the* same Lord *rules* over all, rich among all who invoke Him.

10:13 *omnis enim quicumque invocaverit nomen Domini salvus erit*

For whoever will invoke *the* Lord's name will be made secure.

An Evangelistic Imperative
10:14 *quomodo ergo invocabunt in quem non crediderunt aut quomodo credent ei quem non audierunt quomodo autem audient sine praedicante*

How, then, will they invoke in One whom they have not believed? Or how will they believe in Him of whom they have not heard? But how will they hear without preaching?

10:15 *quomodo vero praedicabunt nisi mittantur sicut scriptum est quam speciosi pedes evangelizantium pacem evangelizantium bona*

How, indeed, will they preach, unless they are sent? As is written, "How beautiful *the* feet of those telling good news of peace, of those telling good news of good!"[29]

The Fact of Disobedience
10:16 *sed non omnes oboedierunt evangelio Esaias enim dicit Domine quis credidit auditui nostro*

Yet not all have obeyed *the* good news. For Isaiah says, "Lord, who has believed by hearing us?"[30]

10:17 *ergo fides ex auditu auditus autem per verbum Christi*

Therefore, faith *comes* from hearing, but hearing *comes* through Christ's word.

10:18 *sed dico numquid non audierunt et quidem in omnem terram exiit sonus eorum et in fines orbis terrae verba eorum*

Yet I say, have they not heard? And, indeed, "Their sound has gone out into all *the* land, and their words

---

[29] See Isaiah 52:7.

[30] See Isaiah 53:1.

to *the* limits of *the* land's circle."[31]

Have They Not Known?

10:19 *sed dico numquid Israhel non cognovit primus Moses dicit ego ad aemulationem vos adducam in non gentem in gentem insipientem in iram vos mittam*

Yet I say, has Israel not known? First, Moses says, "I will lead you to envy against those who are not *a* nation. I will cast you into anger against *a* foolish people."[32]

10:20 *Esaias autem audet et dicit inventus sum non quaerentibus me palam apparui his qui me non interrogabant*

But Isaiah dares and says, "I am found by those not seeking Me. I have appeared openly to those who did not ask about Me."[33]

10:21 *ad Israhel autem dicit tota die expandi manus meas ad populum non credentem et contradicentem*

---

[31] Compare to Vulgate Psalm 18:5.

[32] See Deuteronomy 32:21.

[33] See Isaiah 65:1.

But he says to Israel, "All day I stretched out My hands to *an* unbelieving and contradicting people."[34]

---

[34] See Isaiah 65:2.

Has God Rejected His People?
Romans 11:1   *dico ergo numquid reppulit Deus populum suum absit nam et ego Israhelita sum ex semine Abraham tribu Beniamin*

Therefore I say, God hasn't rejected His people, has He?   Far be it!   For I also am Israelite, from Abraham's seed, Benjamin's tribe.

11:2   *non reppulit Deus plebem suam quam praesciit an nescitis in Helia quid dicit scriptura quemadmodum interpellat Deum adversus Israhel*

God has not rejected His people whom He knew in advance.   Or do you not know what scripture says in Elijah, in what way he objects before God against Israel?

11:3   *Domine prophetas tuos occiderunt altaria tua suffoderunt et ego relictus sum solus et quaerunt animam meam*

"Lord, they have killed Your prophets, thrown down Your altars, and I alone am left. And they are seeking my soul!"[35]

---

[35] See 1 Kings 19:14.

11:4 *sed quid dicit illi responsum divinum reliqui mihi septem milia virorum qui non curvaverunt genu Baal*

Yet what does *the* divine response say to him? "Seven thousand men are left to Me who have not bent *the* knee to Baal."[36]

11:5 *sic ergo et in hoc tempore reliquiae secundum electionem gratiae factae sunt*

So also therefore, in this season, *a* remnant has been made according to grace's election.

11:6 *si autem gratia non ex operibus alioquin gratia iam non est gratia*

But if by grace, not by works! Otherwise, grace already is not grace.

11:7 *quid ergo quod quaerebat Israhel hoc non est consecutus electio autem consecuta est ceteri vero excaecati sunt*

What, then? What Israel sought, this he has not obtained. But *the* chosen has obtained *it*. Indeed,

---

[36] 1 Kings 19:18.

others have been blinded.

11:8 *sicut scriptum est dedit illis Deus spiritum conpunctionis oculos ut non videant et aures ut non audiant usque in hodiernum diem*

As is written, "God has given them remorse's spirit: eyes that may not see and ears that may not hear, even to the present day."[37]

11:9 *et David dicit fiat mensa eorum in laqueum et in captionem et in scandalum et in retributionem illis*

And David says, "Let their table be made into *a* trap and into captivity and into scandal and into revenge to them!

11:10 *obscurentur oculi eorum ne videant et dorsum illorum semper incurva*

"Let their eyes be clouded so they may not see, and their back always bent down."[38]

---

[37] Compare to Deuteronomy 29:4, Isaiah 6:9, Jeremiah 5:21.

[38] See Psalm 69:22-23.

Have They Offended So As To Fall?

11:11 *dico ergo numquid sic offenderunt ut caderent absit sed illorum delicto salus gentibus ut illos aemulentur*

I say, therefore, have they offended so that they fall? Far be it! But their offense *means* security to nations, that they may envy them.

11:12 *quod si delictum illorum divitiae sunt mundi et deminutio eorum divitiae gentium quanto magis plenitudo eorum*

Yet if their offenses are *the* world's riches, and their reduction *the* nations' riches, how much more their fullness!

11:13 *vobis enim dico gentibus quamdiu quidem ego sum gentium apostolus ministerium meum honorificabo*

For I say to you among *the* nations, as long indeed as I am *an* apostle to nations, I will honor my ministry –

11:14 *si quo modo ad aemulandum provocem carnem meam et salvos faciam aliquos ex illis*

if, somehow, I may provoke my flesh to envy, and

make some from among them secure.

11:15 *si enim amissio eorum reconciliatio est mundi quae adsumptio nisi vita ex mortuis*

For if their loss *is the* world's reconciliation, what *will* their adoption *be* other than life from *the* dead?

11:16 *quod si delibatio sancta est et massa et si radix sancta et rami*

For if *the* first fruit is holy, *the* mass *is* also. And if *the* root is holy, *the* branches *are* too.

Parable of the Olive Tree
11:17 *quod si aliqui ex ramis fracti sunt tu autem cum oleaster esses insertus es in illis et socius radicis et pinguidinis olivae factus es*

What if some of *the* branches are broken off, but you, when you were *a* wild olive-tree, were ingrafted among them, and have become *the* companion of *the* root and *the* olive's fatness?

11:18 *noli gloriari adversus ramos quod si gloriaris non tu radicem portas sed radix te*

Do not boast against *the* branches! Yet if you boast,

you don't carry *the* root, but *the* root *carries* you.

11:19 *dices ergo fracti sunt rami ut ego inserar*

You will say, then, 'Branches were broken off so I could be ingrafted.'

11:20 *bene propter incredulitatem fracti sunt tu autem fide stas noli altum sapere sed time*

Well! They were broken off because of unbelief, but you are standing by faith. Don't understand proudly, but fear!

11:21 *si enim Deus naturalibus ramis non pepercit ne forte nec tibi parcat*

For if God has not spared natural branches, neither perhaps may He spare you.

Goodness and Severity
11:22 *vide ergo bonitatem et severitatem Dei in eos quidem qui ceciderunt severitatem in te autem bonitatem Dei si permanseris in bonitate alioquin et tu excideris*

See, then, God's goodness and severity – severity, indeed, among them, but God's goodness among you, if you remain in goodness. Otherwise, you too will be cut down.

11:23 *sed et illi si non permanserint in incredulitate inserentur potens est enim Deus iterum inserere illos*

Yet they also, if they do not remain in unbelief, will be ingrafted – for God is mighty to ingraft them again.

11:24 *nam si tu ex naturali excisus es oleastro et contra naturam insertus es in bonam olivam quanto magis hii secundum naturam inserentur suae olivae*

For if you by nature were cut from *a* wild olive-tree and, against nature, were ingrafted into *a* good olive, how much more will those according to nature be ingrafted into their *own* olive tree!

Don't Be Ignorant
11:25 *nolo enim vos ignorare fratres mysterium hoc ut non sitis vobis ipsis sapientes quia caecitas ex parte contigit in Israhel donec plenitudo gentium intraret*

For I don't want you ignorant, brothers, of this mystery, that you not be wise in yourselves: that blindness has fallen in part among Israel until *the* fullness of nations has entered.

11:26 *et sic omnis Israhel salvus fieret sicut scriptum est veniet ex Sion qui eripiat avertet impietates ab Iacob*

And so all Israel will be made secure, as is written: "He who can rescue will come from Sion. He will turn lawlessness away from Jacob.

11:27 *et hoc illis a me testamentum cum abstulero peccata eorum*

"And this *will be a* testament to them from Me, when I take away their sins."[39]

11:28 *secundum evangelium quidem inimici propter vos secundum electionem autem carissimi propter patres*

According to good news, indeed, *they are* enemies for your sake. But according to election, *they are* most beloved for *the* fathers' sake,

11:29 *sine paenitentia enim sunt dona et vocatio Dei*

for God's gifts and calling are without regret.

---

[39] Compare to Isaiah 59:20-21.

You Have Obtained Mercy

11:30 *sicut enim aliquando et vos non credidistis Deo nunc autem misericordiam consecuti estis propter illorum incredulitatem*

For as at one time you also did not believe God, but now you have obtained mercy because of their unbelief,

11:31 *ita et isti nunc non crediderunt in vestram misericordiam ut et ipsi misericordiam consequantur*

so also they now have not believed to your mercy, so they also may obtain mercy.

11:32 *conclusit enim Deus omnia in incredulitatem ut omnium misereatur*

For God has closed all in unbelief, so He may have mercy on all.

Paul's Doxology

11:33 *o altitudo divitiarum sapientiae et scientiae Dei quam inconprehensibilia sunt iudicia eius et investigabiles viae eius*

O, *the* height of God's riches, wisdom, and knowledge! How incomprehensible are His judgments and unsearchable His ways!

11:34 *quis enim cognovit sensum Domini aut quis consiliarius eius fuit*

For who has known *the* Lord's sense, or who was His counselor?

11:35 *aut quis prior dedit illi et retribuetur ei*

Or who gave to Him before, and it may be repaid to him?

11:36 *quoniam ex ipso et per ipsum et in ipso omnia ipsi gloria in saecula amen*

For from Him and through Him and in Him *are* all *things*! Glory to Him in *the* age! Amen.

Living, Holy Offerings

Romans 12:1 *obsecro itaque vos fratres per misericordiam Dei ut exhibeatis corpora vestra hostiam viventem sanctam Deo placentem rationabile obsequium vestrum*

So I pray you, brothers, by God's mercy, that you display your bodies *as* living, holy offerings, pleasing to God, your reasonable consideration.

12:2 *et nolite conformari huic saeculo sed reformamini in novitate sensus vestri ut probetis quae sit voluntas Dei bona et placens et perfecta*

And do not be conformed to this age, but be reformed in *the* newness of your sense, so you may prove what is God's good and pleasing and perfect will.

12:3 *dico enim per gratiam quae data est mihi omnibus qui sunt inter vos non plus sapere quam oportet sapere sed sapere ad sobrietatem unicuique sicut Deus divisit mensuram fidei*

For I say through grace that is given to me to all who are among you, not to understand more than ought to be understood, but to understand each one with sobriety, as God has divided faith's measure.

Many Members

12:4 *sicut enim in uno corpore multa membra habemus omnia autem membra non eundem actum habent*

For just as we have many members in one body, but all members do not have *the* same act,

12:5 *ita multi unum corpus sumus in Christo singuli autem alter alterius membra*

so we, many, are one body in Christ, but each one members of one another,

12:6 *habentes autem donationes secundum gratiam quae data est nobis differentes sive prophetiam secundum rationem fidei*

but, having different gifts according to *the* grace that is given to us – whether prophecy, according to faith's reason;

12:7 *sive ministerium in ministrando sive qui docet in doctrina*

whether ministry, in ministering; whether one who teaches, in doctrine;

12:8 *qui exhortatur in exhortando qui tribuit in simplicitate qui praeest in sollicitudine qui miseretur in hilaritate*

who exhorts, in exhortation; who gives, in simplicity; who governs, in concern; who has mercy, in cheerfulness.

12:9 *dilectio sine simulatione odientes malum adherentes bono*

Let delight *be* without envy, hating harm, holding fast to good;

12:10 *caritatem fraternitatis invicem diligentes honore invicem praevenientes*

in brotherhood's affection, cherishing one another, outdoing one another in honor;

12:11 *sollicitudine non pigri spiritu ferventes Domino servientes*

not lazy in concern, fervent in spirit, serving *the* Lord;

12:12 *spe gaudentes in tribulatione patientes orationi instantes* rejoicing in hope, patient in trouble, instant in prayer;

12:13 *necessitatibus sanctorum communicantes hospitalitatem sectantes*

communicating *the* holy ones' needs, pursuing hospitality.

Bless Those Persecuting
12:14 *benedicite persequentibus benedicite et nolite maledicere*

Bless those persecuting! Bless, and do not curse!

12:15 *gaudere cum gaudentibus flere cum flentibus*

Rejoice with *the* rejoicing, weep with *the* weeping,

12:16 *id ipsum invicem sentientes non alta sapientes sed humilibus consentientes nolite esse prudentes apud vosmet ipsos*

feeling *the* same thing among each other, not knowing high *things*, but consenting to *the* humble. Don't be wise in your own *opinion* –

12:17 *nulli malum pro malo reddentes providentes bona non tantum coram Deo sed etiam coram* *omnibus hominibus*

paying back no one harm for harm, providing good
not only before God, but even before all men.

Live At Peace
12:18 *si fieri potest quod ex vobis est cum omnibus
hominibus pacem habentes*

If it can be done, that which is from you, having
peace with all men –

12:19 *non vosmet ipsos defendentes carissimi sed
date locum irae scriptum est enim mihi vindictam ego
retribuam dicit Dominus*

not defending yourselves, most loved, but give
anger's place! For it is written, "'Revenge is mine.
I will repay,' *the* Lord says."[40]

12:20 *sed si esurierit inimicus tuus ciba illum si sitit
potum da illi hoc enim faciens carbones ignis
congeres super caput eius*

But, "If your enemy is hungry, feed him. If he thirsts,
give him *a* drink. For doing this, you will gather

---

[40] See Deuteronomy 32:35.

burning coals over his head."[41]

12:21 *noli vinci a malo sed vince in bono malum*

Do not be overcome by harm, yet overcome harm in good.

---

[41] See Proverbs 25:21-22.

Be Subject

Romans   13:1   *omnis   anima   potestatibus sublimioribus subdita sit non est enim potestas nisi a Deo quae autem sunt a Deo ordinatae sunt*

Let every soul be subject to higher powers, for no power exists except from God. But what powers exist were ordered by God.

13:2   *itaque qui resistit potestati Dei ordinationi resistit qui autem resistunt ipsi sibi damnationem adquirunt*

So also, who resists, resists *a* power of God's ordering. But those who resist acquire damnation for themselves.

13:3   *nam principes non sunt timori boni operis sed mali vis autem non timere potestatem bonum fac et habebis laudem ex illa*

For princes are not *causes of* fear to those doing good, but harm. Do you want to not fear power? Do good are you will have praise from it.

13:4   *Dei enim minister est tibi in bonum si autem male feceris time non enim sine causa gladium portat Dei enim minister est vindex in iram ei qui malum* *agit*

For he is God's minister to you in good. But if you work harmfully, fear, for he does not carry *the* sword without reason. For he is God's minister for vengeance in wrath to *one* who carries on in harm.

13:5 *ideo necessitate subditi estote non solum propter iram sed et propter conscientiam*

For this reason, be subject by necessity – not only because of wrath, but also because of conscience.

Pay Your Debts
13:6 *ideo enim et tributa praestatis ministri enim Dei sunt in hoc ipsum servientes*

For therefore also you pay taxes, for they are God's ministers, serving Him in this.

13:7 *reddite omnibus debita cui tributum tributum cui vectigal vectigal cui timorem timorem cui honorem honorem*

Repay debts to all: to whom tax, tax; to whom revenue, revenue; to whom fear, fear; to whom honor, honor.

13:8 *nemini quicquam debeatis nisi ut invicem diligatis qui enim diligit proximum legem implevit*

May you owe nothing to anyone except that you cherish one another, for who cherishes *a* neighbor has fulfilled *the* law.

13:9 *nam non adulterabis non occides non furaberis non concupisces et si quod est aliud mandatum in hoc verbo instauratur diliges proximum tuum tamquam te ipsum*

For 'You will not commit adultery', 'You will not kill', 'You will not steal', 'You will not lust', and whatever is another commandment, it is repeated in this word: "Delight in your neighbor, as in yourself."

13:10 *dilectio proximo malum non operatur plenitudo ergo legis est dilectio*

Delight in neighbor works no harm. Therefore delight is *the* law's fulfillment.

What Time Is It?
13:11 *et hoc scientes tempus quia hora est iam nos de somno surgere nunc enim propior est nostra salus quam cum credidimus*

And, knowing this time, that *the* hour is already *here* for us to rise up from sleep, for our security is nearer than when we *first* believed.

13:12 *nox praecessit dies autem adpropiavit abiciamus ergo opera tenebrarum et induamur arma lucis*

Night has passed, yet day has come close. Let us, therefore, throw off works of darkness and dress in light's armor.

13:13 *sicut in die honeste ambulemus non in comesationibus et ebrietatibus non in cubilibus et inpudicitiis non in contentione et aemulatione*

Let us walk honestly, as in *the* day, not in feasting and drunkenness, not in sleeping around and in sexual impurity, not in contention and envy.

13:14 *sed induite Dominum Iesum Christum et carnis curam ne feceritis in desideriis*

Yet dress yourself in *the* Lord Jesus Christ, and you will not make care for *the* flesh, in lusts.

Bear With the Weak

Romans 14:1 *infirmum autem in fide adsumite non in disceptationibus cogitationum*

Take up *the* weak in faith, but not to disputes about opinions.

14:2 *alius enim credit manducare omnia qui autem infirmus est holus*

For one trusts to eat all, but another who *is* weak eats vegetables.

14:3 *is qui manducat non manducantem non spernat et qui non manducat manducantem non iudicet Deus enim illum adsumpsit*

Let one who eats not despise one not eating, and let *one* who does not eat not judge *one* eating – for God has taken him up.

14:4 *tu quis es qui iudices alienum servum suo domino stat aut cadit stabit autem potens est enim Deus statuere illum*

You, who are you who would judge another's slave? He stands of falls before his own master. But he will stand, for God is mighty to make him stand.

14:5 *nam alius iudicat diem plus inter diem alius iudicat omnem diem unusquisque in suo sensu abundet*

For one regards one day as more than another day. Another regards every day. Let each one be rich in his *own* sense.

14:6 *qui sapit diem Domino sapit et qui manducat Domino manducat gratias enim agit Deo et qui non manducat Domino non manducat et gratias agit Deo*

Who knows *a* day, knows it to *the* Lord, and who eats, eats to *the* Lord, for he gives thanks to God. And one who does not eat, does not eat to *the* Lord, and he gives thanks to God.

Living To God
14:7 *nemo enim nostrum sibi vivit et nemo sibi moritur*

For none of us lives to himself, and none dies to himself.

14:8 *sive enim vivimus Domino vivimus sive morimur Domino morimur sive ergo vivimus sive morimur Domini sumus*

For if we live, we live to *the* Lord. If we die, we die to *the* Lord. Therefore, whether we live or we die, we are *the* Lord's.

14:9 *in hoc enim Christus et mortuus est et revixit ut et mortuorum et vivorum dominetur*

For in this Christ also has died and lived again, so He may be Lord of *the* dead and *the* living.

Why Do You Judge?

14:10 *tu autem quid iudicas fratrem tuum aut tu quare spernis fratrem tuum omnes enim stabimus ante tribunal Dei*

But why do you judge your brother, or why do you despise your brother? For we all will stand before God's judgment court.

14:11 *scriptum est enim vivo ego dicit Dominus quoniam mihi flectet omne genu et omnis lingua confitebitur Deo*

For it is written, "'I live,' *the* Lord says. 'For every knee will bow to Me, and every tongue will confess to God.'"[42]

---

[42] See Isaiah 45:24.

14:12 *itaque unusquisque nostrum pro se rationem reddet Deo*

So also each one of us will return *an* accounting to God for ourselves.

14:13 *non ergo amplius invicem iudicemus sed hoc iudicate magis ne ponatis offendiculum fratri vel scandalum*

Therefore, let us no more judge each other, yet judge more in this – that you not put *a* stumbling block or scandal before *a* brother!

Nothing Unclean In Itself

14:14 *scio et confido in Domino Iesu quia nihil commune per ipsum nisi ei qui existimat quid commune esse illi commune est*

I know and am confident in *the* Lord Jesus that nothing is common in itself, except to one who considers it *so*. What seems common to him is common.

14:15 *si enim propter cibum frater tuus contristatur iam non secundum caritatem ambulas noli cibo tuo illum perdere pro quo Christus mortuus est*

For if your brother is saddened because of food, you are already not walking according to affection. Do not destroy by your food him for whom Christ died!

14:16 *non ergo blasphemetur bonum nostrum*

Therefore, may our good not be reviled.

Fairness and Peace and Joy

14:17 *non est regnum Dei esca et potus sed iustitia et pax et gaudium in Spiritu Sancto*

God's reign is not food and drink, but fairness and peace and joy in Holy Spirit.

14:18 *qui enim in hoc servit Christo placet Deo et probatus est hominibus*

For who serves Christ in this pleases God and is approved by men.

14:19 *itaque quae pacis sunt sectemur et quae aedificationis sunt in invicem*

So also, let us pursue what *things* are of peace, and what are of building up among each other.

14:20 *noli propter escam destruere opus Dei omnia*

quidem munda sunt sed malum est homini qui per offendiculum manducat

Do not destroy God's work on account of food. All things indeed are clean, yet it is harmful to *a* man who through *a* cause of offense *yet* eats.

14:21 *bonum est non manducare carnem et non bibere vinum neque in quo frater tuus offendit aut scandalizatur aut infirmatur*

It is good not to eat meat or drink wine or *do* anything else in which your brother may be offended or scandalized or weakened.

Who Is Blessed?
14:22 *tu fidem habes penes temet ipsum habe coram Deo beatus qui non iudicat semet ipsum in eo quo probat*

You have faith? Have it inside yourself, before God! *One* who does not judge himself in that which he approves *is* blessed.

14:23 *qui autem discernit si manducaverit damnatus est quia non ex fide omne autem quod non ex fide peccatum est*

But *one* who discerns this is condemned if he eats, because *it is* not from faith. But all that *is* not from faith is sin.

Sustain the Weaker

Romans 15:1 *debemus autem nos firmiores inbecillitates infirmorum sustinere et non nobis placere*

But we stronger ones ought to sustain *the* weaker ones' weaknesses, and not please ourselves.

15:2 *unusquisque vestrum proximo suo placeat in bonum ad aedificationem*

Let each one of you please his neighbor in good, to build up.

15:3 *etenim Christus non sibi placuit sed sicut scriptum est inproperia inproperantium tibi ceciderunt super me*

For Christ also did not please himself, but, as is written, "*The* taunts of those insulting you have fallen on me."[43]

15:4 *quaecumque enim scripta sunt ad nostram doctrinam scripta sunt ut per patientiam et consolationem scripturarum spem habeamus*

---

[43] Psalm 69:9.

For whatever *words* are written, are written to our teaching, so that we may have hope through *the* patience and consolation of scriptures.

15:5 *Deus autem patientiae et solacii det vobis id ipsum sapere in alterutrum secundum Iesum Christum*

But may *the* God of all patience and solace give you to know one another in one manner, according to Jesus Christ,

15:6 *ut unianimes uno ore honorificetis Deum et Patrem Domini nostri Iesu Christi*

that, as one, you may honor with one mouth *the* God and Father of our Lord Jesus Christ.

Receive As Christ Received You

15:7 *propter quod suscipite invicem sicut et Christus suscepit vos in honorem Dei*

Because of this, receive each other as Christ also has received you, in God's honor.

15:8 *dico enim Christum Iesum ministrum fuisse circumcisionis propter veritatem Dei ad confirmandas promissiones patrum*

For I say Christ Jesus *was* *a* servant to *the* circumcision according to God's truth, to *the* confirming of *the* fathers' promises;

15:9 *gentes autem super misericordiam honorare Deum sicut scriptum est propter hoc confitebor tibi in gentibus et nomini tuo cantabo*

but to nations, above mercy, to honor God – as is written, "Because of this, I will confess to You among nations, and I will sing Your name."[44]

15:10 *et iterum dicit laetamini gentes cum plebe eius*

And again it says, "Rejoice, nations, with His people!"

15:11 *et iterum laudate omnes gentes Dominum et magnificate eum omnes populi*

And again, "Praise *the* Lord, all nations, and magnify Him, all people!"[45]

15:12 *et rursus Esaias ait erit radix Iesse et qui*

---

[44] See Psalm 18:49.

[45] See Psalm 117:1.

exsurget regere gentes in eo gentes sperabunt

And once more Isaiah said, "*A* root will be to Jesse also, who will rise up to rule nations. Nations will hope in him."[46]

May Hope's God

15:13 *Deus autem spei repleat vos omni gaudio et pace in credendo ut abundetis in spe in virtute Spiritus Sancti*

But may hope's God fill you with all joy and peace in believing, so you may overflow in hope, in Holy Spirit's power.

15:14 *certus sum autem fratres mei et ego ipse de vobis quoniam et ipsi pleni estis dilectione repleti omni scientia ita ut possitis alterutrum monere*

But I am certain about you, my brothers – I myself also – that you also are full of delight, filled completely with knowledge, so that you may admonish one another.

15:15 *audacius autem scripsi vobis fratres ex parte tamquam in memoriam vos reducens propter gratiam*

---

[46] See Isaiah 11:1, 10.

quae data est mihi a Deo

But I have written you boldly in part, brothers, as it were bringing you to memory, according to *the* grace that was given me from God,

15:16 *ut sim minister Christi Iesu in gentibus sanctificans evangelium Dei ut fiat oblatio gentium accepta sanctificata in Spiritu Sancto*

so I may be Christ Jesus's minister among nations, sanctifying God's good news, so *the* nations' offering may be acceptable and holy in Holy Spirit.

Paul's Glory
15:17 *habeo igitur gloriam in Christo Iesu ad Deum*

Therefore, I have glory in Christ Jesus to God.

15:18 *non enim audeo aliquid loqui eorum quae per me non effecit Christus in oboedientiam gentium verbo et factis*

For I do not dare to talk about anything else of theirs that Christ has not brought about through me to *the* nations' obedience by word and act,

15:19 *in virtute signorum et prodigiorum in virtute*

Spiritus Sancti ita ut ab Hierusalem per circuitum usque in Illyricum repleverim evangelium Christi

in *the* might of signs and wonders, in *the* Holy Spirit's might, so that from Jerusalem all around even to Illyricum I might complete Christ's good news.

Paul's Ministry Strategy

15:20 *sic autem hoc praedicavi evangelium non ubi nominatus est Christus ne super alienum fundamentum aedificarem*

So also I have preached *the* good news where Christ was not named, so that I might not build on another's foundation.

15:21 *sed sicut scriptum est quibus non est adnuntiatum de eo videbunt et qui non audierunt intellegent*

Yet, as is written, "Those who were not told about Him will see, and *those* who have not heard will understand."[47]

15:22 *propter quod et inpediebar plurimum venire ad vos*

---

[47] Isaiah 52:15.

Because of that also I was hindered much from coming to you.

15:23 *nunc vero ulterius locum non habens in his regionibus cupiditatem autem habens veniendi ad vos ex multis iam annis*

Now, though, not having another place in those regions, but having *the* desire to come to you already for many years,

15:24 *cum in Hispaniam proficisci coepero spero quod praeteriens videam vos et a vobis deducar illuc si vobis primum ex parte fruitus fuero*

when I begin to set out to Spain, I hope that, passing by, I may see you, and may be sent there from you – if first, in part, I will have enjoyed you.

Going to Jerusalem
15:25 *nunc igitur proficiscar in Hierusalem ministrare sanctis*

Now, though, I am going to Jerusalem to minister to *the* holy ones.

15:26 *probaverunt enim Macedonia et Achaia conlationem aliquam facere in pauperes sanctorum* *qui sunt in Hierusalem*

For Macedonia and Achaia have approved *an* offering, to do something for *the* poor among *the* holy ones who are in Jerusalem.

15:27 *placuit enim eis et debitores sunt eorum nam si spiritalium eorum participes facti sunt gentiles debent et in carnalibus ministrare eis*

For it pleased them, and they are their debtors. For if those of *the* nations have become participants in their spirit, they ought also to minister to them in their flesh.

15:28 *hoc igitur cum consummavero et adsignavero eis fructum hunc proficiscar per vos in Hispaniam*

Therefore, when I have completed this and signed over to them this fruit, I will set out through you to Spain.

15:29 *scio autem quoniam veniens ad vos in abundantia benedictionis Christi veniam*

But I know that, coming to you, I will come in *the* abundance of Christ's blessing.

15:30 *obsecro igitur vos fratres per Dominum nostrum Iesum Christum et per caritatem Spiritus ut adiuvetis me in orationibus pro me ad Deum*

I pray you, therefore, brothers, through our Lord Jesus Christ and through Spirit's favor, that you help me in prayers for me to God,

15:31 *ut liberer ab infidelibus qui sunt in Iudaea et obsequii mei oblatio accepta fiat in Hierosolyma sanctis*

that I may be free from *the* faithless ones who are in Judea, and that *the* offering of my consideration may be acceptable among Jerusalem's holy ones –

15:32 *ut veniam ad vos in gaudio per voluntatem Dei et refrigerer vobiscum*

so I may come to you in joy, through God's will, and be refreshed with you.

15:33 *Deus autem pacis sit cum omnibus vobis amen*

But *the* God of peace be with you all. Amen.

I Commend to You

Romans 16:1 *commendo autem vobis Phoebem sororem nostram quae est in ministerio ecclesiae quae est Cenchris*

But I commend to you our sister Phoebe, who is in *the* gathering's ministry that is in Cenchrea,

16:2 *ut eam suscipiatis in Domino digne sanctis et adsistatis ei in quocumque negotio vestri indiguerit etenim ipsa quoque adstitit multis et mihi ipsi*

that you may receive her in *the* Lord worthily of holy ones, and help her in whatever she may lack in *her* business among you – for she likewise has helped many, including me personally.

Salutations

16:3 *salutate Priscam et Aquilam adiutores meos in Christo Iesu*

Salute Prisca and Aquila, my helpers in Christ,

16:4 *qui pro anima mea suas cervices subposuerunt quibus non solus ego gratias ago sed et cunctae ecclesiae gentium*

who laid down *their* necks for my soul, to whom not

only I give thanks, but also all *the* nations' gatherings,

16:5 *et domesticam eorum ecclesiam salutate Ephaenetum dilectum mihi qui est primitivus Asiae in Christo*

and their native gathering. Salute Ephaenetus, my beloved, who is Asia's first fruits in Christ!

16:6 *salutate Mariam quae multum laboravit in vobis*

Salute Mary, who has labored much among you!

16:7 *salutate Andronicum et Iuniam cognatos et concaptivos meos qui sunt nobiles in apostolis qui et ante me fuerunt in Christo*

Salute Andronicus and Junius, my kinsmen and fellow captives, who are nobles among *the* apostles, who also were before me in Christ!

16:8 *salutate Ampliatum dilectissimum mihi in Domino*

Salute Ampliatus, most beloved to me in *the* Lord!

16:9 *salutate Urbanum adiutorem nostrum in Christo et Stachyn dilectum meum*

Salute Urbanus, our helper in Christ, and Stachys, my beloved!

16:10 *salutate Apellen probum in Christo*

Salute Apelles, approved in Christ!

16:11 *salutate eos qui sunt ex Aristoboli salutate Herodionem cognatum meum salutate eos qui sunt ex Narcissi qui sunt in Domino*

Salute those who are from Aristobolus! Salute Herodionus, my kinsman! Salute those who are from Narcissus, who are in *the* Lord!

16:12 *salutate Tryfenam et Tryfosam quae laborant in Domino salutate Persidam carissimam quae multum laboravit in Domino*

Salute Tryfena and Tryfosa, who labor in *the* Lord! Salute Persida, most beloved, who has labored much in *the* Lord!

16:13 *salutate Rufum electum in Domino et matrem eius et meam*

Salute Rufus, chosen in *the* Lord, and his mother and mine!

16:14   *salutate Asyncritum Flegonta Hermen Patrobam Hermam et qui cum eis sunt fratres*

Salute Asyncritus, Flegonta, Hermes, Patrobas, Herma, and those brothers who are with them!

16:15   *salutate Filologum et Iuliam Nereum et sororem eius et Olympiadem et omnes qui cum eis sunt sanctos*

Salute Filologus and Julia, Nereus and his sister, and Olympiadus and all with them who are holy ones.

16:16   *salutate invicem in osculo sancto salutant vos omnes ecclesiae Christi*

Salute one another with *a* holy kiss!   All Christ's assemblies salute you.

Beware!

16:17   *rogo autem vos fratres ut observetis eos qui dissensiones et offendicula praeter doctrinam quam vos didicistis faciunt et declinate ab illis*

But I pray you, brothers, that you watch those who are working dissensions and offenses contrary to *the* doctrine which you have learned, and turn away from them!

16:18 *huiusmodi enim Christo Domino nostro non serviunt sed suo ventri et per dulces sermones et benedictiones seducunt corda innocentium*

For such as these are not serving our Lord Christ, but their own belly. And they are seducing innocent hearts through sweet words and blessings.

16:19 *vestra enim oboedientia in omnem locum divulgata est gaudeo igitur in vobis sed volo vos sapientes esse in bono et simplices in malo*

For your obedience is told in every place. Therefore, I rejoice in you, yet I want you to be wise in good and simple in harm.

Peace's God

16:20 *Deus autem pacis conteret Satanan sub pedibus vestris velociter gratia Domini nostri Iesu Christi vobiscum*

But peace's God will crush Satan quickly under your feet. *The* grace of our Lord Jesus Christ *is* with you.

16:21 *salutat vos Timotheus adiutor meus et Lucius et Iason et Sosipater cognati mei*

Timothy, my helper, salutes you, and Lucius, and

Jason, and Sosipater, my kinsman.

16:22 *saluto vos ego Tertius qui scripsi epistulam in Domino*

I, Tertius, who wrote *the* letter, salute you in *the* Lord.

16:23 *salutat vos Gaius hospes meus et universae ecclesiae salutat vos Erastus arcarius civitatis et Quartus frater*

Gaius, my host, salutes you, and *the* whole gathering salutes you, *with* Erastus, the city's treasurer, and brother Quartus.

(Verse 24 is missing in the Latin)

Benediction

16:25 *ei autem qui potens est vos confirmare iuxta evangelium meum et praedicationem Iesu Christi secundum revelationem mysterii temporibus aeternis taciti*

But to Him who is mighty to strengthen you, according to my good news and *the* preaching of Jesus Christ, according to *the* mystery's unveiling, kept quiet through eternal ages,

16:26 *quod nunc patefactum est per scripturas prophetarum secundum praeceptum aeterni Dei ad oboeditionem fidei in cunctis gentibus cognito*

that now is made known through prophetic writings, according to God's eternal commandment, to faith's obedience, recognized among all nations,

16:27 *solo sapienti Deo per Iesum Christum cui honor in saecula saeculorum amen*

to *the* only wise God through Jesus Christ, *be* honor in *the* age of ages. Amen.

Also in **The Latin Testament Project**

The Way of Wisdom: Job, Proverbs, Ecclesiastes, Song of Solomon (English and Latin-English Editions), 2008

The Audacity of Prayer: A Fresh Translation of the Book of Psalms (English and Latin-English Editions), 2009

The Jagged Edge of Forever: Deuteronomy, Daniel, The Minor Prophets (English Edition), 2009

Beginnings: A Fresh Translation of Genesis (Latin-English Edition), 2009

The Latin Torah: Fresh Translations of Genesis, Exodus, Leviticus, Numbers, Deuteronomy (Latin-English Edition), 2010

Pastoral and General Epistles from the New Testament: A Latin-English, Verse-by-Verse Translation (Latin-English Edition), 2010

The Gospel According to Mark: A Latin-English, Verse by Verse Translation (Latin-English Edition), 2010

The Latin Torah: English Edition with Commentary 2011

Searchlight Press
Who are you looking for?
Publishers of thoughtful Christian books since 1994.
info@Searchlight-Press.com
www.Searchlight-Press.com
www.JohnCunyus.com

www.ingramcontent.com/pod-product-compliance
Lightning Source LLC
Chambersburg PA
CBHW031556040426
42452CB00006B/324